PURPOSEFUL
PAIN

LAUREN GRIMES-JACKSON

Cover photography by AG Imagery
Front cover designed by Don Carey III
Back cover designed by The Joyous Marketing Team
Editing by Self-Publishing Services

Printed in the United States of America

First Printing: June 2019

ISBN- 978-1-7331182-0-0

MY PURPOSE

As you're about to enter Purposeful Pain, it is important that you know that this book was written not only to assist you in navigating towards the finding of your purpose, but also to lead you into an intimate and lasting relationship with Christ, the Rock that is higher than I.

DEDICATION

I dedicate this book first to my idol, Harriet Tubman, as one who left and returned on purpose to free hundreds of slaves. My design is to do the same, after having been set free, laying bare my life experiences in an effort to set at liberty the broken and lead them to wholeness and purpose.

Further, I dedicate this book to my "whys," my two young sons, Alan D. Jackson, III, and Alex Lawrence Jackson. This healing was for the two of you!

To my mother, who spent COUNTLESS hours editing, reading, transcribing, and praying through it all. This book would be nothing without you! I love you beyond the stars, and I am so grateful for your God-given gifts.

To my father, thank you for instilling in me to never allow the throws of life to determine the fate of my destiny. Thank you for reminding me daily that I was always built for this moment, on PURPOSE.

TABLE OF CONTENTS

FOREWORD

Hello Pain,

I am pretty sure you are surprised to see me smiling wider, looking better, and slaying my goals. I decided to write to you and thank you for all you did to get me to this point. There were so many times on this journey when I questioned what God's plan was in burdening me with your constant presence, but I finally understand the reason God had you there all this time—so I could experience Purposeful Pain.

Experiencing Purposeful Pain has been like delivering a baby and enjoying all of the emotional rollercoasters that come along with hormonal changes. There were days when I felt horrible, wanting to give up and never come out of my room. Then there were days when I felt as if the world was my domain and there was nothing stopping me from reaching all my lofty goals. Lastly came the fear of delivering this baby alone. Could I truly see this thing to the end? Did God intend for it to be like this?

But God positioned me to hear Him and learn about my Purpose so I could teach the world how to live a WHOLE life built upon living with Purpose for the glory of God. So, Pain, thank you for helping me to find my Purpose and for readying me for the next dimension. Truth be told, I wasn't ready, but I am now!

Onward with Purpose,
Lauren

PUTTING A NAME
TO THE PAIN

I f you have been intrigued enough to open this book, you must have experienced pain at some point in your life. My desire, as my life unfolds before your very eyes in this book, is to bring you to the realization that pain is designed to make you better, not bitter.

Wikipedia Dictionary defines pain as, "Physical suffering or discomfort caused by illness or injury." However, pain can manifest itself in many different forms other than physical. Emotional pain forms the backdrop of this book, and it is defined by Elizabeth Bolger as, "A state of feeling broken that involved the experience of being wounded, loss of self, disconnection, and critical awareness of one's more negative attributes."[1]

Many of us have labored under emotional distress, and most have emotional wounds that have not yet healed. Throughout the discourse of *Purposeful Pain*, you will travel with me, Lauren G. Jackson, a woman who has survived the vagaries of emotional trauma in her journey toward wholeness. I hope that through my pain, you can find healing.

Let the journey begin!

---

[1] Elizabeth A. Bolger, "Grounded Theory Analysis of Emotional Pain," in *Psychotherapy Research, 1999; 9:342-362 (Nov. 2010).*

At twenty, I became a wife to a wonderful man whom I met in college, and at twenty-four, our first child was born. My career in the banking industry was taking off, and I was experiencing tremendous success. With plenty of education—two master's degrees and a bachelor's degree—I was on top of the world!

At this young age, I had even accomplished home ownership. I was living the American dream and felt God had placed me right where I was destined to be. Everything around me seemed to be flourishing, until the brokenness of my childhood returned to haunt my life. At that point, I found out who I was and who I was meant to become.

As a wife, I was controlling, and worst of all, I did not know how to allow my husband to be the head of our home. Truth was, I did not grow up seeing this type of husband-and-wife dynamic. My parents were married, but the roles of husband and wife appeared to be reversed. As a result, I had no idea what expectations came with the title "wife." I believed my husband and I were a team, and we would conquer the world together. I had not experienced what it was like to be led as opposed to being the leader, how to openly communicate, or even how to be vulnerable. I didn't know these things were the basis of a harmonious relationship.

Truthfully, I was still the little girl who was angry with her father for dismantling her family with his own brokenness. It was hard for a seven-year-old Daddy's girl to accept that he was not perfect.

I was no stranger to conflict, as my parents had often engaged in verbal disputes, but one particular incident caused a rift that lasted decades. I overheard my father having a conversation with another adult, and I was upset by what he was saying. I told my mother about the conversation I'd heard, and she confronted my father. My father blamed me from that moment on for repeating what I had overheard. It was evident that the anger he felt turned into bitterness and ultimately resentment toward me. Our relationship was never the same. I resented my father for reacting so strongly, and I resented my mother for putting me in *grown folk's* business. Although I did not truly understand all the demons plaguing our family, I certainly felt the impact.

Here I was, a married woman carrying the fragments of a broken child inside. I had no idea how to heal that little girl inside, and, even worse, I didn't know how to communicate that I was still hurting. All I knew was that I never wanted to be wounded that badly again. I wanted love, but I wanted to control how and when I felt it. I wanted peace, but I was not at peace with myself. I wanted a healthy relationship, but I had no clue how to have one. I had many desires, but lack of courage and faith crippled me and stifled my emotional growth.

My belief that controlling everything around me was the only way I could manage pain was, in and of itself, painful. Oh, but that was a lie! A lie I spent many years telling myself, and, worst of all, wounding myself in the process. Looking back, I would tell my younger self, "You were too broken to be a wife."

At the time, I believed I was ready to wear the title of "Mrs." even though I was young and the union was against my father's wishes. The more my dad expressed his displeasure with my getting married, the more determined I became to do just that. I had to prove to him, yet again, that I would be successful with or without his support. What I did not understand was that my dad had married my mom when he was only twenty-one. He had likely been nowhere near ready to be a husband or father, nor assume the overall responsibility for a household.

I had fallen into the same trap, a trap he had been trying to protect me from—the trap of thinking, "I am grown, and know what I am doing." My resentment of him deafened me to his insights. In retrospect, I wish I would have listened to him and taken the time to get to know myself as well as the person I wanted to spend the rest of my life with. Instead, I found myself jumping into matrimony headfirst.

Alas, I listened to no one and marched to the beat of my own drum. Contrary to popular belief, especially that of my father, I would one day create a *model* family. In my mind, I had indeed been successful in fashioning a life that mirrored the family I had grown up in. My *model* family consisted of a successful daddy, a successful mommy, children, a nice house, great careers, good values, and regular church attendance.

From the outside, my adult family seemed to have it all together. But the perfect life was an illusion. Although it appeared that I had everything, I still did not have peace, joy, respect, and loyalty—those intangible things that create a successful relationship and happy life. Instead, I was reliving the emotional brokenness from my childhood, but this time I was the wife (as was my mom) who had to decide to either stay or go. The mistakes I blamed my mother for making were the same ones I was waking up to every day. From my vantage point, my mother never held my father to a level of accountability for his actions that ultimately led to the demise of our happy home.

It was not until I decided to give up my will in exchange for God's that I began to see purpose in my pain. I had to embrace Jesus's statement: "And we know that all things work together for good to them that love God, to them who are the called according to His purpose." (Romans 8:28)

Healing can never be realized until the source of the pain is identified and remedied. After much soul-searching, I was able to discover that *self-preservation* was the cause of my pain. I was living my life by the adage, "Only the strong survive!" Self-preservation caused me to build emotional walls around my heart, and I endeavored to live my life on the defense.

As a child, my flaws were constantly being highlighted by my father, and his flaws were constantly being highlighted by me. Imagine growing up only wanting the approval of your father. For a young girl, this type of deficit makes her question, "What about me is unworthy of your love?" and leads to the idea that, "Maybe if I prove that I'm worth loving, then I will receive the love I so desire."

I had limited power to change my father's heart. Everything I did, I wanted to be the absolute best, so then he could finally be proud of me. In academics, I was always at the top of my class, receiving the most and highest honors from elementary school all the way up to high school. I even graduated high school as a junior. I remember hoping this would make my dad proud of me, but my hopes went unfulfilled. He expressed to me that I was growing up too fast and was not ready to head to college—especially one three hours away from home. My dad had no idea that I wanted to be as far away from home as was humanly possible.

And, I realized, I was tired of trying to prove myself. This was the moment I put up my "wall of Jericho" around my heart. It was imperative that I fortify my heart so as to preserve my sanity. My favorite scripture at the time was, "And, ye fathers, provoke not your children to wrath: but bring them up in the nurture and admonition of the Lord." (Ephesians 6:4)

In my marriage, perhaps the biggest complaint my husband had was that I never allowed him to be the leader of our home. He even went so far as to say to me one day, "Lauren, I want to feel like the man in our home." Understand, readers, that as a child my perception was that my mom had assumed the leadership role in our family. She appeared to be the "go-to guy."

My husband desired my submissiveness, but had he earned that right to make such a demand? In hindsight, certainly not by his ways and actions. Consequently, I would tear him down verbally, when, truthfully, I was afraid to trust him because he had disappointed me so many times before. That feeling of disappointment was one I knew all too well.

The idea of someone leading me was scary because I would have had to relinquish control and operate in vulnerability. Becoming vulnerable requires being whole and comfortable in your own skin. Unresolved pain resulted in my being emotionally unavailable and unable to facilitate an environment that would make my husband feel important and needed, and the man I so desired him to be.

So, here I was at thirty-one, with two kids, going through a divorce, and the time had come for me to do some true healing and find out what God's perfect will was for my imperfect life. To begin this process, I had to stop beating myself up about my mistakes, and I had to give myself permission to walk around lost until I found the courage to fully examine old wounds and find my purpose.

Now that I am finally able to open up and be transparent concerning the pain that has plagued me for years, I feel a strong sense of liberation. Perhaps the most important lesson I have learned is that though we experience pain, we will survive. Pain is inherent to the birthing process of a better you.

It is so important to allow people to be the best that they can be, based on who they are. For those of you who are struggling with a relationship, ask yourself if you can accept your partner or spouse for who they truly are, not for who you want to them to be. If you find that you can't accept the actual person, their character defects considered, then perhaps you're not in the right relationship. Please don't be afraid to let go of someone or something that may be toxic or just not the right fit in the grand scheme of things. Trust the process of becoming *equally* yoked. Trust God to show you your Boaz! Boaz, in the Bible, was a wealthy and prominent man who allowed a lowly peasant woman to glean in his fields, collecting leftover grain to survive. Boaz was hopelessly smitten by this woman named Ruth and left extra grain in his field just for her. Yes, Boaz favored her, kept other men from even addressing her, and finally took her as his bride. This beautiful story is recorded in Ruth, Chapter 2.

This whole process of purposeful pain resulting in divorce is hard—devastating, even. However, the only way to grow is to become accountable for the brokenness you brought into the relationship and to understand its role in your relationship's failings.

Turn to your *Purposeful Pain* prayer journal. Below are questions and thought-provoking statements that I urge you to answer as a means of documenting and diagnosing your pain:

- Put a name to your pain.
- What compels you to go back to the place of turmoil, a place you might have thought you left behind?
- What is the addiction that compels you to retreat into the very thing God never ordained for your life in the first place? What's love got to do with it?

Here are thoughts to ponder as you journal:

- It's scary to say, "I've been abandoned," "I've been abused," "I've been let down!" Often, we don't want to put a name to those sources of pain because doing so makes those situations a reality, and we can't ignore the long-term effects anymore.
- Abuse, abandonment, addiction—they become real! But you have to acknowledge the true reason for your pain, so that, should history repeat itself, you will not fall into the same trap as before.

Defining and naming your pain will help you to navigate through this world in such a way that not only will you be able to forgive the person who hurt you, but forgive yourself for how you reacted to the hurt.

Isn't it amazing that, even with all the evil things we, as people do, God extends to us His unmerited, undeserved grace? As you embark upon naming the pain, keep in mind the grace that you've been afforded. Resolve to become a better person in light of your pain instead of bitter because of it. Moving forward, I urge you to meditate on Psalm 116:5: "Gracious is the Lord, and righteous; yea, our God is merciful."

Transparency

My first introduction to pain was one that made me question, "Lord, haven't I been through enough? Why me?" And then I heard the Lord say, "Why not you?"

I can recall being the only little girl at prayer service in my grandparents' house listening to the old folks sing hymns and meters and pray fervently. I can remember my grandfather praying and calling God, "a healer, a mind regulator, and a way out of no way," and he started his prayer off with so much conviction, as if he truly had seen God's hand move just in this way.

God took me back to that moment when I asked why had I been betrayed, and what good could come from all this brokenness. Then he reminded me of the scripture, "It is good for me that I have been afflicted; that I might learn thy statutes." (Psalms 119:71 KJV)

As a little girl, hearing these prayers and these scriptures didn't mean much to me. However, today they are the words and prayers I rest on.

How could I pray like my grandparents and know with everything in me that God is a healer unless I needed His healing touch? How else would I know Him to be a mind regulator, unless I needed Him to keep me in perfect peace? And how would I know Him to make a way out of no way, unless I found myself in a hopeless situation, crying out "Hosanna?"

WHO DID IT?

Think about a moment when you were a child, maybe when you were out playing with friends, and one of them struck you. It likely ended when you ran to your mom and said: "Mommy, *so-and-so* hurt me," and you pointed out the culprit.

Now, think about this same scenario as an adult. You're in pain, and you're hurting. You may have lost your best friend, you may have had a tragedy happen in your life, you may have lost a job, you may have ended the marriage, or you may have lost yourself. There are times when you're riddled with pain, and you find yourself wondering who it is at fault. Especially because it's easier to blame others. But what happens when the one "who did it" is you?

Sometimes our expectations are what pain us. The greatest disappointment we will ever face is when we expect someone to operate at a level that is far beyond their ability.

Let's visit one of your most painful moments and think about the expectations that accompanied them. Maybe you expected that *he/she* was going to show up. You expected they would do all the things they promised, but then they didn't. The next time, you're a little more perturbed, a little more agitated, but you give them another chance. Then, as luck would have it, it happens another time. What is the old saying? "Fool me once, shame on you. Fool me twice, shame on me."

Often when we are consistently letdown by mankind, we find ourselves expecting the same of God, almost as if we believe He too will fail us. My dears, the Bible warns in Psalm 118:8, "It is better to trust in the LORD than to put confidence in man."

When I met my ex-husband, I liked him, but I was immediately intimidated by him because he was older. I was intrigued by his fancy car and his zest for life, and I believed he was going to be super successful. I fell in love with the ideal of him. But, at that moment, I never thought we would have a future. It was always a running joke between my ex-husband and I that he had a way with the ladies. He was in a fraternity, so you can only imagine his persona.

Looking back, had I paid attention to his character, I would not have been as surprised or as hurt as I am by the decisions he made during our relationship. But I was blinded by my baggage and my desires, and I ignored the pit in my stomach when we continued to have arguments about the same thing, i.e., his entertainment of other women.

I couldn't understand why I always felt as if I was in competition for his heart. Again and again, I found myself trying to prove my worthiness of love and loyalty, just as I had done with my father.

If you never fix what is broken, it is inevitable that you will re-experience what broke you. That was very true in my case. My husband needed validation and constant praise, and I needed to feel worthy of love. These issues resulted in a cycle that continued for the next eleven years of our marriage. We were two very passionate people, in love, and neither one of us ever unpacked our pain bags.

As I go through this arduous process, as I deal with the unraveling of the life that I've made, I ask myself so many times, "Who did it?

Were there moments where I could have blamed my spouse for the ultimate demise of our marriage? Most definitely. But as I reflect on where I've been and where I'm headed, I must say that I was at fault for the failure of my marriage as well, for: (a) not unpacking my pain bag, (b) failing to recognize the character traits my mate possessed, and (c) not asking God to send me the husband of His choosing.

Ultimately, because of our failed relationship, I found myself carrying even heavier bags and having to unload them alone. My husband had been in my life since the age of seventeen; I literally built my home in him. Now that he's no longer in my life, I have found my strength in God. My testimony is such that, "I will lift up mine eyes unto the hills from whence cometh my help. My help cometh from the LORD, who made heaven and earth." (Psalm 121:1-2)

I'm no longer left with the question of "who did it" because I have come to accept the part that I played in the grand scheme of things. I was powerless over the person my husband was at his core, yet I chose to believe that my love and loyalty to him would be enough to change him. Oh, how wrong I was! My expectations were predicated upon the belief that one day I would receive all the love, respect, loyalty, and worth that I had longed for, as long as I could endure it as he morphed into the man God had designed him to be. Unfortunately, I was only a part of his journey and would never reap the benefits of the finished product.

It was not given to me to heal my husband of the wounds left by his past, wounds that left him looking for other salves. And, in the end, his choices—and my choices—left me shattered.

Transparency

Here is my truth and personal reflection: I had to learn how to trust God. I always wanted to build up my faith and relationship with Him, but I did not understand at the time how faith would be built.

I thought a consistent, daily prayer time would help me feel as if I was developing a relationship with God, but I was so wrong. I did not understand how this process of building a relationship with God was going to work until He allowed trouble to arise in my life. I literally became desperate for Him.

In the past, I prayed to God. I was a preacher's kid, so I grew up in the church, listening to scriptures and doctrines, going to Bible study, vacation Bible school, and church services. But it was not until I had no one else to trust but God that I began to nurture the seed that had been planted in me since I was a little girl.

He taught me how to develop proper expectations and prepared me for this journey to wholeness. I am not saying that changing my viewpoints on expectations happened overnight, but I found the pain more bearable if I managed my expectations. God warned me of the pitfalls ahead, all the while showing me how I would overcome them should I fall prey to them.

God is our hero! He wants us to lean and depend on Him and trust Him. Trust me. I understand trusting God requires a level of vulnerability and relinquishing of control on our part that can be very scary. However, Isaiah 55:11 offers this assurance from our Lord: "So shall My word be that goes forth from My mouth; It shall not return to Me void, But it shall accomplish what I please, And it shall prosper in the thing for which I sent it." God does not make empty promises. Whatever He has promised us will come to pass.

Understanding "who did it" and where to place proper expectations and blame is crucial to your healing. All the things we endure are not always someone else's fault. People show us who they are by how they treat those they claim to care about. However, the enemy has a way of deceiving us into believing we can influence change in a person. We can impact someone's life so as to invoke change, but this is not always the case. People will not magically make a change because you have joined their lives.

When you enter into any type of relationship, you need to ask yourself:

- Does this connection bring glory to God?
- Can God's purpose for my life be realized with this person around?

Only prayer and fasting will bring the answer to you. Just make sure that when God gives you revelatory knowledge concerning the aforementioned questions, you do not ignore such knowledge for your own selfish reasons.

If we learn how to manage our expectations for man and God, we will truly reach our purpose. Take some time to meditate on this scripture: "In all thy ways acknowledge Him, and he shall direct thy paths." (Proverbs 3:6 KJV)

LOSSES VERSUS LESSONS

Have you ever found yourself thanking God for losses that turned into lessons? I've had those moments many times. I've even declared I will never live another day with loss; instead, I look for the lesson.

When you learn to look for lessons, you find purpose, wholeness, and peace. It is then that you will be able to unlock the next level of transformation that God has ordained for your life. The task becomes elevating your mind past your personal hurt, so that you can embrace God's plan for your incremental development along with incremental elevation.

Once I decided that I was going to search for lessons in the midst of my "losses," it completely changed the way I viewed my life and other peoples' lives as well. We're all on this journey together, and we're all trying to do God's will and live the best lives we can.

All too often, the reason we can't truly live our "best life"— according to God's design—is because we can't accept the lessons. We're so consumed with our losses, the people and things we have left behind, that we can't even see that God has created something new in us. Therefore, we find ourselves bogged down in the losses and negativity, and we can't get ahead. But it's all a mind game.

Remember, losses do not define who you are; they are simply what you went through. God reminds us that "as a man thinketh in his heart, so is he." (Proverbs 23:7) What you believe about yourself dictates what you see and manifest into reality.

In your time of journaling, address the following:

- What are you saying about yourself when you're going through your losses?
- Let's not call them losses anymore. Instead, call them "sheddings" or the "shedding season."
- Who are you telling yourself that you are?
- Was there ever a time that you told yourself that you are strong, that you will get past whatever is troubling you, or that your latter life will be greater?

The enemy (used interchangeably with the devil) knows that if he can stifle you in your losses, you will never get to lessons, and, therefore, never get to purpose. So, he sends your friends or your "frenemies" to come and relay a message of gloom and doom. Most often, the devil sends the people you're closest to. They could even be your parents. These people may say things that make you question God and who He says you are, as well as where you are headed.

Therefore, it behooves you to be very mindful when you're in your shedding season. Make sure those you allow to speak into your spirit are sent by God. The wrong information from the wrong source can completely derail your ability to heal and become whole.

You need people around you when shedding: those who can coddle you in prayer, clothe you with positivity, and gift you with God's Word and promises. Often, they are the people whom you never expected God to send. But that's what God does—He sends us misfits.

He may send the solution to your problem from the mouth of a babe. The Psalmist illustrates this thought: "Out of the mouth of babes and sucklings hast thou ordained strength because of thine enemies that thou mightest still the enemy and the avenger." (Psalms 8:2) God uses whom He chooses to deliver His message of hope in the midst of despair.

Often, we expect the soundest advice to come from seasoned Christians. Yet the young and inexperienced persons, babes in Christ, can be remarkably wise.

God reminds us He wants to see us free and happy. His plans for us are not built on negativity and pain, but on promise and hope. He experienced the ultimate pain when He gave His Son. God portrayed the ultimate example of pain, loss, and lessons when His Son was sent to the cross. Yes, He lost His Son in order that we might gain eternal life.

When you can say, "God, I bless you, for the losses are going to turn into lessons and allow people to see the *you* in me and not the *me* in me," you'll find yourself on the road to recovery and wholeness.

I'm reminded of a little song my mother taught me as a child: "I'm a little teapot short and stout, here is my handle, here is my spout. When I get all steamed up, hear me shout. Just tip me over and pour me out!" In other words, our plea to God should be: "Lord, empty me of me and fill me with you."

Allow God to cut away things in your life that are not of Him. Embrace God's pruning process. John 15:2 describes that process: "Every branch in me that bears not fruit he takes away; and every branch that bears fruit, he purges it, that it may bring forth more fruit."

Transparency

When I was twenty-one years old, my ex-husband and I moved to the city. There was a neighborhood we were in love with. We rode through it all the time, never conceiving we would one day live in that neighborhood, but God had a plan!

My ex-husband and I sacrificed and worked, and, by the grace of God, we purchased property in our dream neighborhood and started building a home. That was the first time that I truly understood the scripture: "No weapon that is formed against thee shall prosper; and every tongue that shall rise against thee in judgment thou shalt condemn." (Isaiah 54:17, KJV)

The building process seemed to be the longest ever. My ex-husband went to the building site every single day. Upon completion, our home was in the "Parade of Homes." It was magical. No one could have convinced me my life wasn't a gift from God.

Soon, we welcomed our second child. At the time, I believed this was the home we would raise our children in, watch them drive out of the garage in their first car, have many parties and birthdays… This was going to be our house of love, our house of protection, and our forever home.

And yet, instead of it being my safe place, it became my cellblock as our marriage deteriorated. I felt trapped by this thing called love! When God leaves your heart and your home, it doesn't matter how big or beautiful your home may be; ultimately, it will become your prison.

The hardest part of going through a divorce is the unraveling of the life that you and your spouse have sacrificed blood, sweat, and tears to acquire and maintain.

As a result of our pending divorce, our dream home was placed on the market. I must admit every single time there was a showing of my house to a potential buyer, I hated it. It drained all my energy. It stung of failure. It also reminded me of our sacrifices for what had been our home.

In these vulnerable moments, God reminded me that I might be bruised, but I was not broken, and all that He began in me would manifest. Those things that I found myself crying over were only distractions and tactics of the enemy. Divorce, by its very nature, is a severing of ties among people as well as possessions.

As providence would have it, my dream home was sold to the highest bidder. But by letting go of my dreams, the chains that bound me were stripped away, and I was freed to follow God's plan for my life.

As I go through my phases of grief and mourning, I am reminded that connected to every loss is a lesson, and every lesson gives birth to purpose. It is human to grieve over the losses we endure, but it is Christ-like to weep with the knowledge that this too shall pass.

God reminds us, "that weeping may endure for a night *but* joy cometh in the morning." (Psalms 30:5 KJV)

And, in Haggai 2:9: "The glory of this latter house shall be greater than of the former, saith the Lord of hosts: and in this place, will I give peace, saith the Lord of hosts."

So, while I was so overwhelmed with the loss of my home that I loved so much, God was saying, "Child, come on and trust me. You're worrying about a house that you helped to build when I'm trying to give you the promise (as written in Joshua 24:13 KJV): "And I have given you a land for which ye did not labour, and cities which ye built not, and ye dwell in them; of the vineyards and oliveyards which ye planted not do ye eat."

NECESSARY

So, what if I told you that the trials I encountered on the road to wholeness were necessary? It has been said that we must learn to trust God's heart even when we can't trace His hand.

God knows how much we can bear, whether we are willing to go through the process or not. Pain is a motivating factor—no pain, no gain! This chapter is designed to help you to begin to see life in such a way that you don't get upset about the necessary pain but, rather, become grateful for the pain.

When you think about pregnancy and the timeframe that it takes for a baby to go from a little seed, to getting its first organs, to the development of its skin, bones, and muscles, you know all of this is necessary. And so, in the season of necessary, you must realize God is performing the miracle of life inside of you, so that in due time you will introduce to the world that which God has ordained.

By my very nature, I am a fighter. And yet, when my ex-husband and I became separated, and life and my enemies struck blow after blow, I remember crying out to God and saying, "God, is all of this necessary?" When I was broke, "God, is it necessary? Do I have to be this broke? Do I have to start at this level? I'm hitting a glass ceiling on my job; is that necessary?"

I found myself having to learn how to wiggle and move through the politics of corporate America. Work was frustrating. Home life was frustrating. My world seemed to be crumbling, and there was nothing I could do to stop it. My marriage had taken a nosedive and fallen headlong into divorce.

Finally, I became comfortable saying that I was going through a divorce. Initially, expressing this was very daunting because, for me, the very idea of divorce represented failure. And I wanted the fantasy of "living happily ever after" in which I had been promised.

Now, thanks to God, instead of feeling broke, busted, and disgusted, I find myself *fuller* of life than ever before. God's grace and mercy, coupled with the prayers of the righteous and wise counsel, served to undergird me and shore me up. I leaned heavily upon Philippians 4:13: "I can do all things through Christ which strengthened me."

Divorce freed me from the lashes of infidelity, which I had endured for many years of my marriage. Freedom makes me glow from the inside out, while providing me the sense of being my most fearless self!

When I was married, I became the vision of who my ex-husband thought I *should* be. But now that my covering is gone, I am now able to define who I am becoming—without outside influence. I'm able to just be *me* and follow God's perfect plan. Jeremiah proclaims God alone knows the plans He has for each of us, to prosper us and to give us hope. (Jeremiah 29:11)

Looking back, my marriage was not all bad. There were a lot of high points and some low points, but it served a greater purpose. I needed the lessons this experience afforded me. All of the heartache, pain, excitement, joy, and partnership, and all the goals that were set and conquered served to catapult me in the arms of God. I'm excited about where I'm headed. And so, when things come up that give me pause— like my youngest son going to pre-K, a moment my husband and I would have shared had we remained in covenant—God reminds me things are as they should be.

Though the images for your future may be distorted, trust in God and the knowledge that there's greater ahead. When you've conquered something, that thing can no longer define you. For example, I'm not afraid of being vulnerable because I've experienced the pain caused by invulnerability. My only regret is that I wish I had let go of all of the things I feared and trusted God earlier; He was guiding me through necessary lessons.

When a man comes into my life, the first thing I let them know is: "Look, Boo, before you sit at this table and try to talk to me, know that talking to me will require some things. Because of who I am in Christ and what He has deposited in me, I'm going to change your life. I might help to increase your credit score. I might help you reach a goal you thought unattainable, all because I'm a life changer. I'm going to pray for you. I'm going to be your biggest supporter, and I'm going to mandate that you love me as God loved the church. And I'm not going to accept just anything, or the bare minimum… Here are the standards. You're going to have to know how to treasure me—my heart is delicate."

I think the problem for a lot of women who have gone through hurt is that the experience has not allowed us to remain delicate. Our pain forced us to become concrete, and we're so full of concrete pain that we can't allow anything to grow in the soil of our souls. Nothing grows because our soil is no longer conducive for planting.

What can grow through concrete?

Weeds.

And what do weeds do?

Weeds suffocate and kill.

Weeds in a flower bed will choke the very life out of your flowers. Flowers are dainty. They are vulnerable. And so, as women, our concrete souls are the reason we can't submit to our spouses.

God makes our soul like a rich soil; he makes us engaging and a conducive place for true love to grow. And He can reduce even the thickest of concrete back into earth through time and necessary changes.

Thank God for the necessary changes in our lives; these temporary pains help us harvest our purpose.

Perhaps you needed that relationship to be severed. You needed him/her to cheat on you. You needed him/her to tell you that you weren't good enough. You needed him/her to tell you, "Yes, you're okay, but so-and-so is better." You needed that because all of those moments prepared you. It was all necessary. And so, when you accept the necessary vagaries of life, you become unstoppable. And everything the world says you can't become, you shall become, because you've endured the pain and came out victorious.

Let me give you another great example of a process that is necessary: working out. It is necessary for our health. There are all these health plans, health kicks, and different things to do to get healthy; but working out, although it is not fun, is also essential. I have a bachelor's degree in Health and Exercise Science, and I do *not* like exercising. I look fit, but I don't like the process because it takes discipline, it takes consistency, and it makes you change your eating habits. All of those things put together lend themselves to accountability. But the results are amazing.

Change hurts, especially in the beginning of this new phase of life. Your body hurts because it's doing something it has never done before. I am writing this book to assist you in doing something you've never done before. I want you to go against the grain—to go against what man and the world says, and begin to learn how to see people and occurrences in your life differently so you don't remain in bondage.

The only person who doesn't want to see you elevated is the person who's okay with you being as low as they are. I recommend you check your circle of friends. If you find your circle of friends applauding you only when you're in the same sinking boat, so to speak, as they are, versus when you're attempting to rise above adversity, it may be time you begin the process of ridding your life of them.

When you can't stand your mate, and you're posting questionable stuff on social media to take digs at that person, look at the people cheering you on. Look at the people who applaud you when you turn to your ex and say, "I love you. But I love you enough to know I can't be with you and maintain respect for you." Those applauding you for taking the elevated path are those whom you should keep in your life. Not the people who ask, "Does that mean you want him back?" They don't understand that you don't want him back; you just don't want him to be broken.

In my case, we have two young boys who look up to their father. They need him to be the best version of himself, a version that does not exist with me in his life.

Even though we didn't work out, I still pray and cover him. I don't operate in the eyes of offense because the Bible suggests, "Greater is He that is in me than he that is in the world." (1 John 4:4)

I don't live in bitterness or pettiness, and this makes me free. John 8:36 reminds us: "So if the Son sets you free, you will be free indeed." I endeavor to walk in freedom, and that is my earnest desire for all of you who are reading my life's story.

I thank God for my necessaries. God is faithful, He cares, He is always watching, and He is always there. Our Lord rose above His enemies. How was it that He dealt with those who persecuted Him? Hear Him saying, "Father, forgive them, for they know not what they do." (Luke 23:34)

What a perfect example of all things *necessary*!

Transparency

I'm not just shooting from the hip when I speak of the lessons highlighted in this book. God makes me live out each message. And as each chapter unfolds, I'm more and more concerned about what level of elevation He's going to require of me next.

Anytime God reveals something to me, He does so in a vision. Yes, this really happens! While working on this chapter, God gave me a revelation. He showed me a vision of my husband (at the time) walking into a bar with his paramour (side chick), and I was there with my best friend. God was preparing me because—I'm going to be real—I love God, but there are some things that He has not yet delivered me from!

True to my vision, while out at the bar with my best friend that same night, I saw a truck like my husband's pull up outside. Immediately I thought, *Oh, God! Here it is!* The vision was coming to fruition before my very eyes. I silently prayed I was wrong and it was not his truck, but that was to no avail.

Of course, the two of them walked up together. Praise God they weren't holding hands. As they walked in, my husband didn't see me, but his lady friend most definitely did.

Instead of lashing out like a crazy woman, I was filled with peace because God, in His infinite wisdom, had prepared me by way of a vision. The only thing about my vision that bothered me was that I never saw how I would react to seeing the couple together. All I knew was that the man to whom I had given fourteen years of my life would be reveling in his indiscretion in front our peers, and thereby disrespecting me.

How quickly we went from being a "Power Couple" to a "Power Outage."

That night, I had several moments where *she* was near me. I could not utter a word to her for fear it would quickly escalate. However, I spoke to my husband and said "hello." And I held my head high, making them both extremely uncomfortable because of my poise and politeness.

I found strength in the knowledge that God was setting me up to birth my Purpose. He was doing His best work, and God alone would get the glory out of this situation. Until that moment of purposeful pain, I hadn't been sure that I was going to write this testimony and guide for others going through the most humiliating and humbling experiences of life, but thanks to another vision from God, I knew it was my purpose to spread His Word.

In the midst of my second vision, God reminded me how bold the enemy was, even in Bible days. He reminded me of the story of Job as recorded in Job 1:6-7: "One day when the angels came to report to God, Satan, who was the Designated Accuser, came along with them. God singled out Satan and said, 'What have you been up to?' Satan answered God, 'Going here and there, checking things out on earth.'"

In the King James Bible, Satan replies by saying: "I'm walking to and fro, seeking whom I may devour." Satan would look into the eyes of the Creator of both heaven and earth and state his intentions for mankind. Please don't forget that Satan, this "angel of light," had been kicked out of heaven for wanting to *be* God!

The enemy is so cocky and bold that he told God that if He removed the protection He had around Job, he could make Job curse God to his face. But unlike Satan, God knew exactly what type of strength Job carried.

And just like Job, God knew my strength, but the enemy did not. Just as the enemy was not successful in making Job dishonor God, he was not successful in making me dishonor my God or myself. What the enemy did not know was that the pain was validating that God will always come first in my life.

There are not many people who could have handled that situation like I did, especially because I had history with this woman. She had been in my home, pretending to admire me as a woman, but all the while being envious of my life and coveting my husband. Here she was now publicly walking around with him like he was her trophy.

My dear readers, rest assured this story isn't designed to evoke sympathy in you because through it all, I was able to recognize the sovereignty of God in my situation. Just as Joseph encouraged his brothers who had wronged him after the passing of their father, Jacob, not to be fearful that he would retaliate against them for their wrongdoing, I too can rest on Joseph's resolve: "But as for you, you meant evil against me; but God meant it for good, in order to bring it about as it is this day..." (Genesis 50:20).

LIVING THROUGH IT

There will be moments as you go through pain trying to get to purpose that you'll discover a dichotomy inside of you. There is indeed a war brewing between flesh and spirit! Ultimately, Satan's aim is to keep you from reaching the destiny God has ordained for your life. He is intent on disrupting God's plan for you and sabotaging your freedom. Satan can only accomplish his goal if you let him. I write to encourage you, dear readers, to look up and live. Seek God's face all the more!

As you experience purposeful pain, know that what you're going through is truly not about you. Sometimes it's hard for us to hear that, as we want everything to be about us. So, if the enemy can get you to believe *you* are the central focus of your pain, the buck stops with you. Then, my dears, what you're going through will never help others who may be tied to your destiny. There is always somebody watching you, watching your life, and either silently cheering you on as you encounter trials or waiting to see you crumble and fall when you do. I admonish you, grab on to God's unchanging, unwavering hand and allow Him to lead you to victory. It is written: "Yet, in all these things we are more than conquerors through Him who loved us." (Romans 8:37 NKJV)

Living this life requires that you be able to recognize the difference between friends and foes. But, if you ask, God will give you the discernment and the wisdom to know the difference. On the journey toward wholeness, you will be met with many adversities, but stay the course. When things go wrong, hold on to the word of God as recorded in Romans 8:31: "If God be for us, who can be against us?"

Lean also on the words of Psalm 23:4-6 (ESV), where David proclaims: "Even though I walk through the valley of the shadow of death, I will fear no evil, for you are with me; your rod and your staff, they comfort me. You prepare a table before me in the presence of my enemies; you anoint my head with oil; my cup overflows. Surely goodness and mercy shall follow me all the days of my life, and I shall dwell in the house of the LORD forever."

Additionally, you have to be able to "call those things that be not as though they were," (Romans 4:17b) and remind the enemy that if God said it, *it is so.*

In your quest to survive the painful process that leads to wholeness, recognize you're in the biggest battle of your life. You want to react. You want to lash out, to say ugly things, to hurt those who hurt you—an eye for an eye—but God reminds us in Romans 12:19: "Do not take revenge, my dear friends, but leave room for God's wrath, for it is written: 'It is mine to avenge; I will repay,' says the Lord."

Nobody can repay your enemies like God Almighty.

So, as you go through, living through pain, be encouraged, be of good cheer, and speak the Word of God over yourself. It is important you understand that when people attack you, it's not really *you* they're attacking. The attack is really against God and His plan for your life. Most especially, the attack is designed to cause you to abort or abandon the very thing God has strategically deposited within you for the benefit of others. Don't compete where you don't compare!

We forfeit our peace when we try to handle the vagaries of life with our own strength. Hear God saying, "Be still and know that I am God: I will be exalted among the heathen, I will be exalted in the earth." (Psalm 46:10)

I encourage you readers to speak over your situation like you've never spoken before. Guard your ears. Guard your mouth. Satan can't win. God set you up for the win; all you have to do is wake up every day giving Him grace, gratitude, and thankfulness, and be ready to walk in victory.

God never promised us that weapons would not form against us, only that when Satan throws his fiery darts our way, they would not prosper. God's declaration concerning us is recorded in Isaiah 54:17: "No weapon that is formed against thee shall prosper; and every tongue that shall rise against thee in judgment thou shalt condemn. This is the heritage of the servants of the LORD, and their righteousness is of me, saith the LORD."

I don't care what the enemy says your situation looks like. I don't care what the devil's report says. I don't care what the statistics say about your healing. What does God say about your healing? What does God say about your situation? When we listen to what God says about us, it doesn't matter what man says. No, my dears, it matters not what man *says* about you; what matters is what God *knows* about you!

God is not a God who works on man's time. He works on His own time. My grandmother used to say of God, "He's an on-time God, yes He is. He may not come when you want Him, but He'll be there right on time." Satan is relentless in his quest to destroy you, but be like Job in that, come what may, he held on to the God's promises and he received favor.

In this season of "living through it," as challenges come and Satan attempts to buffet you more and more with each passing day, remember to anchor yourself in the LORD. Instead of telling God about your problems, try telling your problems about God!

Transparency

Throughout this process of "Living through it," the most common question I receive from my peers is: "How do you make it through?" The answer is *faith*. My faith has been what has kept my mind in perfect peace, and cultivating my relationship with God has been where I have found rest. My peace mirrors that of Philippians 4:7: "And the peace of God, which passeth all understanding, shall keep your hearts and minds through Christ Jesus."

Often, during our trials and tribulations, our ability to accept the things we cannot change results in us learning how to live through the process. The enemy wants our purpose to die even more than he wants us to perish. People die all the time, but it is their legacy that lives on and continues to effect change in people who may have been lost.

Once I realized what I was living through was embarrassing and hurtful but necessary for God's plan and purpose for my life, I quickly found myself going from victim to victor. My pain was not a mark against me, but a platform for me to use to heal myself and others.

I have encountered many women who have gone through brokenness, divorce, infidelity, and other setbacks and pain, but I have never witnessed any of these women heal. God showed me that it was my purpose to not only heal, but also document how I used His Word to do so. I vowed to God that I would live with intentionality and no longer waste my pain but use it as fuel to take me to my purpose.

Allow me to leave you with one of my favorite passages of Scripture, Psalms 34:19: "Many are the afflictions of the righteous: but the Lord delivereth him out of them all."

FORGIVENESS

Let's talk about forgiveness. You had to know as you perused the pages of this book that at some point we would have to get to this big "F" word that so many people despise.

Forgiveness is an action word and requires discipline, vulnerability, and transparency. The ability to forgive, to be vulnerable, and transparent—especially to those who have hurt or wronged you —is terrifying. But forgiveness is key to being successful in this process of purposeful pain.

Forgiveness is not about the other person; it's about you. It's about using the key of freedom to *unlock* your soul. When someone hurts us, our children, or someone we love, our first reaction is to hurt back. We have a very revengeful and retaliatory spirit. But never allow your pain to keep you captive. With forgiveness comes freedom.

God is a forgiving God, and certainly all of us have been recipients of His forgiveness. Our aim as Christians is to be Christ-like; as such, we should show forth His attributes in how we deal with others.

If there's something you feel like you can't do, chances are that is the very thing you should absolutely be doing. I don't care what that might be. If you feel like you could *never* own a business, you should try to own a business. If you feel like you can't get past childhood hurts, you should actively be working toward forgiveness.

Why? Because the enemy wants us to live and wallow in unforgiveness. There, we are unable to live with purpose or operate in our divine calling from God.

The Bible reminds us that when God forgives us, He throws our sins into the pits of Hell, never bringing them back up again, never rehashing them. We have this promise from our Lord tucked away in Psalms 103:12: "As far as the east is from the west, so far hath He removed our transgressions from us."

Luke 6:35-37 sets forth God's mandate, which should be the Christian's mantra: "But love your enemies, do good to them, and lend to them without expecting to get anything back. Then your reward will be great, and you will be sons of the Most High, because He is kind to the ungrateful and wicked. Be merciful, just as your Father is merciful. Do not judge, and you will not be condemned. Forgive, and you will be forgiven."

Imagine if God rehashed and regurgitated everything you did wrong—like we do in relationships. Think about your last relationship and your current one. How often did/do you act with unforgiveness and resentment? Why not put pen to paper, begin to journal, and recall incidences where you chose not to let "sleeping dogs lie." You'll be surprised how many times you reminded someone of their past, even when you claimed to have forgiven them and wiped the slate clean.

Now, imagine if God acted from the same feeling of resentment. How would you feel? What would our very existence look like? We would probably cease to exist. I am grateful God does not give us what we truly deserve! If He had, our souls would have been hurried to judgment a long time ago. Yet God lengthened out the fragile threads of our lives and bid our golden moments to roll on a little while longer! Where would we be, but for the grace of God?

My dears, oftentimes in the forgiveness process, we have to learn how to forgive ourselves for allowing the pain to happen. Yes, you were hoping for better from your spouse or significant other, even when they showed you what they were really made of. Yes, you chose to turn a deaf ear and a blind eye to the defects in their character. Yes, you made your loved ones out to be what you needed them to be. But forgive yourself. If you don't deal with unresolved issues and are content to sweep them under the rug, you are hiding a monster that will one day rear its ugly head.

Allow me to paint you a picture. So, let's pretend you're back on your first date. Think about how that person made you feel. Probably, you were on cloud nine! Thereafter, you were texting them in the morning; they were calling you all day. They couldn't do their job without thinking about you. You were the apple of their eye. But then *you* showed up, and now you've started to cause them pain. You're like a thorn in their flesh!

Sometimes this scenario is the basis for unforgiveness. We find ourselves falling in love with the "illusion" versus the "reality." After we've been put through pain and hell, we're mad, riddled with unforgiveness, and left carrying emotional bags, right?

I joke all the time, telling my girlfriends, "Southwest only allows you two bags free of charge!"

You can't carry around bags of unforgiveness and wonder why God hasn't freed you. The issue was *you* the entire time. Acknowledge the part you played in the deception process and forgive yourself so that you can forgive your transgressor.

Total freedom from the grips of unforgiveness doesn't show up in the clothes you're wearing or what designer bag you're carrying. These material things are only a disguise that serves to camouflage who you truly are at the core. I'm not saying designer bags aren't awesome; I love a great designer bag. But who are you without the designer? Who are you without the makeup? Who are you without the flashy car? Who are you without the big degrees? Who are you at your core? Are you someone who is caring? Loving? Empathetic? Someone who has the ability to forgive? Someone who has the ability to love even after devastation? Who are you at your core?

Reflect on the most painful lesson you've had to go through and reflect on how you handled it. *Have* you handled it? You may want to record your actions during the process and then grade your own paper. Did you fail miserably or did you pass with flying colors?

Remember, avoidance is not forgiveness. Just because you avoid certain people or situations, that does not mean you are suddenly free. Likely, the person you're avoiding is not even aware that they've wronged you or that you are indeed hurting as a result. Addressing pain is nothing more than self-reflection. You don't have to call every person who has wronged you, and say, "I forgive you." Just allow your actions to reflect forgiveness. How you act is a testament to how you feel and what you feel.

Endeavor, as you muddle through *Purposeful Pain,* to live free of pain, hurt, and unforgiveness. Hebrews 12:1b says, "Let us lay aside every weight, and the sin which doth so easily beset us, and let us run with patience the race that is set before us."

Transparency

As I divulge my thoughts on forgiveness, I am reminded of a popular expression: "I'll forgive, but I won't forget." Another similar expression is: "I'll forgive you, but then I'll deal with you by way of a long-handled spoon." That idea of forgiveness equates to never trusting again and never allowing the trespasser into my personal space again.

I did not fully understand the art of forgiveness until my heart was torn in pieces at the hands of someone who professed to love me. It was then that I understood both the difficulty and necessity of letting go and letting God have the fragments of my broken heart. What I did not realize was that the expression of forgiving but not forgetting was sowing a seed of unforgiveness. The Bible's depiction of forgiveness is a far cry from what this assertion encourages. However, most of us, if we are honest, live by that adage. We can forgive you, but forgetting what you did is like demanding a miracle from a person who does not have the power to change their own circumstance.

Unforgiveness is truly the ultimate bondage that prohibits us from walking into God's purpose for our lives. When I decided unforgiveness was not worth more to me than God's will for my life, I had to actively learn how to not only forgive, but forget.

The story of the three Hebrew boys, Shadrach, Meshach, and Abednego is one that imbues me with hope. In this story, they were placed in a fiery furnace with an audience to watch them suffer. But as the Bible records it, they did not come out looking or smelling like they had literally been tried by the fire. Daniel 3:27 records the encounter as: "And the princes, governors, and captains, and the king's counselors, being gathered together, saw these men, upon whose bodies the fire had no power, nor was a hair of their head singed, neither were their coats changed, nor the smell of fire had passed on them."

After reading the passage, I believed if God could do this for them, He could heal and protect me the same way.

Forgiveness can rest and abide within you when you solicit God's help in that regard. When you come to the end of yourself (relying on your own abilities), you are in the place where you will find God! He is waiting patiently for you to come to the realization as recorded in Philippians 4:13, "I can do all things *through Christ* who strengthens me." Walking upright and favorable with Him will always yield greater dividends than walking in unforgiveness and bitterness.

Just as faith and fear cannot reside together, neither can unforgiveness and wholeness. Choose to be free on PURPOSE!

WORTH VERSUS VALUE: ARE THEY THE SAME?

What are you worth? How much do you value yourself? Those are two questions you need to answer, so I'm going to help you answer them in this chapter. In my quest to do so, I will attempt to dissect the words "worth" and "value," and show you how they fit into our everyday lives. *Worth* is what you're willing to pay for something, such as a home. *Value* is what that home means to you, taking into consideration the maintenance and the upkeep.

You've heard people say, "I can't put a value on that." You've never heard someone say, "I can't put a worth on it." What did you portray about your own self-worth that made you devalue yourself so much so that you allowed others to draw you into a cycle of pain? Do you perceive yourself to be nothing more than a doormat to be trampled upon? Do you do anything to get attention, even if it's negative? Do you always esteem others above yourself? My dear readers, you alone can dictate how you are treated and valued.

Let's talk about the process of buying a car. The majority of the time, the buyer is interested in how much their monthly payments will be. But what if you made your long-term decision based on value, based on the maintenance, what would be required for upkeep of the vehicle? You may not have chosen the car you're riding in today if you knew what it would cost to keep it operable and of value for resale or trade in.

LAUREN GRIMES-JACKSON | 48

The same idea goes into homeownership. People are afraid of homeownership because although they can afford the mortgage, they are hard-pressed to afford the maintenance, cleaning out the flowerbeds, the repairs, the insurance, and the list goes on and on. There's no landlord to call. You are the person responsible by virtue of ownership. It falls on you. Consequently, you find yourself having to discern the difference between monetary worth and personal value.

In relationships, there is an old adage that suggests, "The same way you got them is the same way you will lose them," which is synonymous to, "The same thing it took to get them is the same thing it takes to keep them." In maintaining a healthy relationship, whether that's a marriage or a friendship, you must consistently nurture it and avail yourself to it so as to promote growth and sustenance. You value your relationship just that much. However, no one is expected to compromise to the point of losing their own identity and jeopardizing their own happiness. Recognize the potential toxicity level of the relationship and make an assessment whether or not it is worth buying into for the long haul.

Do you customarily settle for substandard relationships that can only yield substandard commitments? I will admit that I have compromised countless times and found myself looking in the mirror and not recognizing who's looking back at me. Truthfully, the value I once placed on myself was no longer there. Pain will do that to you. Excessive, intensive pain will send you places you thought you'd never go, all because you discounted your own self-worth and depleted your value

What are you saying about your worth and your value? Anything that you value, you will give the utmost care. Remember God, through His Son Jesus, redeemed us by the shedding of His own precious blood. God valued us so much so that when we were in the marketplace of slavery being slaves to sin, He redeemed us from the hands of the enemy, only to satisfy our mouths with good things and fill our souls with His precious Holy Spirit.

We must be careful when we're going through our dark places not to discount our worth and exclude our values. You've done things, you've said things, you're becoming things that are unlike God because you no longer value yourself. This is evident in the way you carry yourself. This could ultimately cost you your life or everything you knew about yourself. You will no longer recognize the person in the mirror!

I can recall a time in my life when I didn't think very much of myself because I was looking at my worth through someone else's eyes. I was seeking validation and looking for love in all the wrong places. Can you relate to what I'm saying? Unmet, unrealistic expectations! I expected someone to value me who didn't know what I was worth. Only God our creator knows our true worth.

As I conclude this chapter, technically there is a difference between value and worth; however, in the eyes of God they are synonymous. My dears, know that the value (the price He was willing to pay for our redemption) placed on us by God was in direct proportion to our worth even while we were yet sinners. God's matchless love for His children has never waned. Psalms 139:13-16 (MSG) gives a beautiful illustration of how and why God values His creation:

Oh yes, you shaped me first inside, then out; you formed me in my mother's womb. I thank you, High God—you're breathtaking! Body and soul, I am marvelously made... You know me inside and out, you know every bone in my body; you know exactly how it was made, bit by bit, how I was sculpted from nothing into something. Like an open book, you watched me grow from conception to birth; all the stages of my life were spread out before you, the days of my life all prepared before I'd even lived one day.

Because of God's love for mankind, He thought we were worth saving, so He purchased us with His own precious blood. Since God our Father has saved us from the power and penalty of sin, justified us, only to one day glorify us, we are invaluable to Him!

FOR MY GOOD

T he Psalmist echoed the sentiments of the Apostle Paul, by proclaiming in Psalms 119:71, "It is good for me that I have been afflicted; that I might learn thy statues." I love that scripture because it is a reminder to all of us that as we go through purposeful pain on our way to our ultimate destiny, instead of giving up, we will realize that along with incremental elevation comes incremental development. There is suffering attached to growth. The Apostle Paul's declaration in Romans 8:28 gives this assurance: "And we know that all things work together for good to them that love God, to them who are the called according to his purpose." It was good that you went through what you went through because in the midst of it you came to know who God is, His precepts and statutes. Now you know your value and worth. Now you know your purpose, all because God valued you enough to allow affliction to mold you into a masterpiece.

Many of us would not be in the place we are today had we not gone through pain. We would never have garnered an appreciation for the things we've acquired, the vocation we now enjoy, or the status in life that we have been afforded had we not been channeled through the wilderness of life to get there. Remember, we can only get to the mountaintop (place of plenty) by way of the valley (place of lack and pruning).

The Bible is replete with striking examples of people who endured hardness and pain in order to come out victorious. Research the life of *Joseph* in Genesis 41:39-42 and see his elevation after his dream was misinterpreted by his siblings. Read the book of *Job* and you'll discover that he lost everything he held dear, yet God blessed him above and beyond his wildest dreams. Job 42:10-12 records in part: "...the Lord restored his fortunes and gave him twice as much as he had before." Consider *Moses* who gave God every excuse not to use him as a liberator of the Israelites, yet he found himself facing Pharaoh and delivering the profound message from God, "Let my people go"! Please read the entire book of Exodus for an appreciation of the life of Moses. There are many others who "went through" but "came through" such as *Paul, Timothy, Peter, John, Gideon,* and the list goes on and on. Most noteworthy is the fact that the cross for *Jesus* represented purposeful pain yet He endured it willingly. Yes, Jesus had His Gethsemane moment where He prayed to His Father, "...if it be possible, let this cup pass from me; nevertheless, not as I will, but as you will" (Matthew 26:39b-ESV).

When we come to the point where we can be grateful for the pain we've encountered and endured, it changes our perception of life. God never promised us flowery beds of ease; instead John 16:33 (ESV) gives both a warning and a promise: "I have said these things to you, that in me you may have peace. In the world you will have tribulation. But take heart; I have overcome the world."

I can recall my mother remarking that God never takes us "to" what He is not able to take us "through". That suggests to me that we should never find ourselves focusing on something that God has already delivered us from. If you ever are determined never to return to the pain you left, you become strategic in how you maneuver and how you allow things to flow in and out of your life. Perhaps formerly, you had an open-door policy, but now your mantra is," Knock before you enter."

You fight harder to maintain what you have because it was not easy to acquire. Your appreciation for something you've had to work for is greater than for that which has been handed to you freely. The Bible says, "For unto whomsoever much is given, to him shall much be required" (Luke 12:48-KJV). The blessings that God bestows upon us are not to be misused or abused. By the same token, God does not expect us to subject ourselves to someone who will mishandle His most prized possession,

YOU! Self-inflicted pain is not purposeful pain that God ordained and allowed for your good. To the contrary, the end product of self-inflicted pain is self-destruction which does not feel good "to" us and is certainly not good "for" us. My advice to you is if you're in a painful situation and you can't see God's hand in it, get out of it!

I would venture to say that not all marriages are of God. The ideal thing to do when contemplating marriage is to ask God to send you a husband or wife after His own heart. Love is a beautiful thing when it is shared with someone who is worthy of that love. If you read the entire chapter of I Corinthians you will discover what love is and what it is not. A marriage that was not God ordained, God inspired or God centered, is not one meant for your good. If you meet an untimely demise because you married a known murdered, the element of goodness for you would be realized when God delivers you from that marriage that was not His doing in the first place. Know that if you are experiencing rejection by a spouse that was not handpicked by God himself for you, that rejection is setting you up for elevation. Perhaps the entire situation was part and parcel of God's divine intervention. Think it not strange when God snatches you from the clutches of a bad marriage or relationship. God may be aligning you for prosperous work and in time you will come to know that your trials were designed to make you strong.

Sometimes God causes people to reject you so that He can push your life toward your purpose. He has to take you through some things to try you and see if you can handle where He's taking you. Rest assured, everything is a training camp for the next blessing.

When we find ourselves questioning, *God, why me? Why now?* Know He is preparing you. Pain is a very real part of that process. Endeavor to plant good seeds in your season of pain because it is all working together for your good.

What we go through is never really about us. Remember Jesus' admonishment to Peter in Luke 22:31-32? "…Behold, Satan hath desired to have you, that he may sift you as wheat: But I have prayed for thee, that thy faith fail not; and when thou art converted, strengthen thy brethren." Someone is depending on you to strengthen them in the midst of their trials and tests. My dear readers, there are some folk who are tied to your destiny and are depending on you to persevere and endure hardness like a good soldier, just as the Apostle Paul admonished young Timothy in II Timothy 2:3.

In this season, allow God's best for you. Seek His face first and foremost. God's desire is that you taste of His blessings that He ordained just for you and be able to say as He said when looking back at His creation, "Umm, that's good!" Heed the clarion call, "Oh, taste and see that the Lord is good" (Psalms 34:8).

As you live, do so purposefully and adhere to the admonishments of James 1:2-3; 12: "My brethren, count it all joy when ye fall into divers temptations; knowing this, that the trying of your faith worketh patience.... Blessed is the man that endureth temptation: for when he is tried, he shall receive the crown of life, which the Lord hath promised to them that love him." You needed those afflictions. You needed to be gracefully broken so that God the potter could put you back together again. Even now, more than ever before, our Heavenly Father wants to blow your mind! Receive of the Lord who is the "...giver of every *good* and perfect gift" (James 1:17).

GIVE ME YOUR ISAAC

L et me tell you a story that is near and dear to my heart. It is the story of an elderly couple in the Bible who were waiting on God to perform a miracle. These two people were none other than Abraham, the father of the faithful, and Sarah, the mother of a nation.

Yet, Sarah was barren. So how could Abraham be called a father and Sarah a mother in the throes of barrenness?

Only God can cause things to *be* although they clearly are *not*. Consider this biblical assertion in Paul's letter to the Romans, Chapter 11:34: "For who has known the mind of the LORD? Or who has become His counsellor?"

Only God, in His infinite wisdom, knows and holds our tomorrow. God never goes back on His word and His promises are sure; however, His timing is not synchronized with our desires. God knew Abraham needed a son so His promise would become a reality, a reality that would affect generations to come, and the barren wife of Abraham would one day conceive.

In the days of Abraham and Sarah, in Israel, barrenness was considered a curse. A woman was considered blessed if she was fruitful, as children were necessary for the perpetuation of the tribes and their religion. Fruitfulness was God's special blessing to His people. In Deuteronomy 7:14, God sets forth the blessings of obedience. This one in particular spoke to the issue that plagued Abraham and Sarah: "You shall be blessed above all peoples; there shall not be a male or female barren among you or among your livestock."

Imagine how Sarah felt. Certainly, she did not feel blessed of the Lord because she remained among the unfruitful. Not only that, but see Abraham's dilemma. At age seventy-five, God promised Abraham in Genesis 12:4 that he would become a "great nation." Would not you have expected that promise to be fulfilled right away if you were in Abraham's shoes?

Hear God speaking in Genesis 15:1: "…the Lord came unto Abram in a vision, saying, Fear not, Abraham: I am thy shield, and thy exceeding great reward." But Abraham poses the question to God: "And Abram said, Lord God, what wilt thou give me, seeing I go childless, and the steward of my house is this Eliezer of Damascus?" (Genesis 15:2) In other words, God, is someone else's seed going to carry on my legacy?

God answers in verses 4-6: "…This shall not be thine heir; but he that shall come forth out of thine own bowels shall be thine heir. And He brought him forth abroad, and said, look now toward heaven, and tell the stars, if thou be able to number them: and He said unto him, So shall thy seed be. And he believed in the Lord; and he counted it to him for righteousness."

God made Abraham a promise, and Abraham believed! God could have made good on His promise instantaneously, but Abraham had to first show himself a worthy vessel, yielding and still. Before blessings can be realized, even in our lives, God has to be convinced our faith will stand the test. It is only when we stand for God in faith that He will stand for us in battle.

Abraham loved Sarah as God loves the church, His bride. Abraham desperately wanted God to make good on His promise, for Sarah's sake as well. Abraham was married to Sarah for many years, even though she carried the stigma of being a cursed woman because of her inability to conceive. Nothing was wrong with Abraham, and we see no account in the Bible of him cheating on Sarah. This does not mean Abraham did not grow impatient. Genesis 15:1-3 bears record that Abraham, ten years after the promise, reminds God that He, in fact, has not kept His promise.

To make the promise more real to Abraham, God actually tells Abraham (in Genesis 17:18-21) that he and Sarah would have a son whose name would be Isaac who would be born at this same time the following year. *God never shows His hand until He's ready to play His hand!*

In the interim, Sarah decides God's promise is laughable at best because she is much too old. Abraham could not be the father of nations without first having fathered a son. Hagar, her handmaid, would be the only woman who could possibly give Abraham what he needed. Abraham took his wife's advice, "went into" Hagar, and she bore him a son named Ishmael.

Sarah's advice worked, but it was not according to God's plan or will for their lives. Sarah later abused Hagar and sent Hagar and Ishmael packing. Such are the consequences of not remaining faithful to God and faithful to your spouse. The consequences of disobeying God are more than meets the eye. Ishmael would later be blessed by God, but he was not the "child of promise."

In Genesis 21, we read about the birth of the promised son, Isaac, whose name means "child of laughter." At the time of his birth, Abraham was one hundred years old and Sarah was ninety-nine. But God kept His promise!

Isn't it amazing how God's keeping of His promises is not contingent upon whether or not we keep our end of the bargain? If God said it, you can count on it.

God's timetable may be different than ours, but we must endeavor to trust Him. Many times, the blessing is held in abeyance because we are not ready to receive it.

God had tested Abraham but now in Genesis 22:1-2, God puts him through the ultimate test, the offering up of Isaac, his only son, on Mount Moriah. This was a test Abraham would not fail! "And it came to pass after these things, that God did tempt Abraham, and said unto him, 'Abraham': and he said, 'Behold here I am.' And he said, 'Take now thy son, thine only son Isaac whom thou lovest, and get thee into the land of Moriah; and offer him there for a burnt offering upon one of the mountains which I will tell thee of.'"

Why such a demand from God? No doubt this demand was part and parcel of the fulfillment of God's promise. Isaac was the only son of Abraham and Sarah, and he was Abraham's beloved son. The main thrust of this sacrifice was made clear in Hebrews 11:18, which says, "In Isaac shall your seed be called."

God did not give Isaac to Abraham and Sarah just as a personal gift. God's intention was to achieve His own goals through Isaac. Abraham followed the excruciating mandates of God. Little Isaac carried the wood, Abraham had the knife and the fire in his hand, but where was the sacrifice? It was Isaac himself.

As Abraham readies Isaac to be sacrificed, the angel of the Lord called to him from heaven: "Do not lay your hand on the lad, or do anything to him; for now I know that you fear God, since you have not withheld your son, your only son, from Me." (Genesis 22:12-NKJV)

As the story goes, Abraham looks behind him and sees a ram caught by its horns in a thicket, takes that ram, and sacrifices it instead.

God provided the ram! He wanted Abraham to garner a deeper relationship with Him and see Him as God the Father! Yes, God had given him Isaac, but not to be worshipped above Him.

See the big picture? Yes, God gives us children to love, nurture, and bring up in the admonition and fear of the Lord, but not to worship. Inasmuch as children are a great gift from God, we are not to put the experience of childbearing and child-rearing before continuous worship and fellowship with God. Remember, God created us for His good pleasure. He wants all of our devotion. He will not be second in our lives. God, our Father, is the only one who will never forsake us.

I love this story so much because it is our reminder of how God can come into covenant with us, and, when we mess up, we can repent and He will take us back into His good graces and bless us.

Now that you've gone through the pain and come out victorious—after having identified the pain, forgiven the source of that pain, and thanked God—you must do the scariest part of this entire process. You must give God the very thing you thought you couldn't live without. Whether it is your husband, your wife, your children, your career, your purpose, your hobby…whatever that thing is in your life that you feel you cannot give over to God, that is the very thing you should feel compelled to relinquish. Follow Abraham's lead and lay your all on the altar of sacrifice before the Lord. What you are holding onto does not compare with what God wants to release to you.

Let's pause right here for a journaling moment!

- Who is your Isaac?
- Are you willing to part with whatever or whomever your Isaac may be in exchange for a relationship with God, your creator and Father? (Isaac was dispensable, but we cannot be separated from the Father even for a moment!)
- If God withdraws Himself from us, where would we be?

Surrender your Isaac to God's able keeping. God is not looking to slay your Isaac, but to have you put God himself in His proper place, first and foremost, in your life. With God as the head of your life, blessings from the windows of heaven will rain down upon you and all those connected to you for generations to come. Your community will be blessed, and everything you touch will be blessed, all because you've come to realize you *can* sacrifice Isaac, but you *cannot* sacrifice God. Ultimately, only what you do for Christ will last!

Transparency

This book has seen me through my darkest days. I have been honored to share my story and allow you to see my life unfold as I navigated through the wilderness.

My hope, when I started writing, was that I would be a comfort to you as you found purpose in your pain. I wanted to make sure you felt me holding your hand through the scary moments, crying with you in the middle of your distress, and celebrating your triumph when you finally understood why God had to take you through the process.

As I close out *Purposeful Pain* and my last transparency, I want you to understand that deciding to file for my divorce was me giving God my Isaac, not giving up, but giving up my will for His will for my life. God set this journey before me, making it evident that I had great works to do and that there were people who needed to see what overcoming looked like. God had to strip everything from me to reverse my course.

Before this purpose occurred, I did not want to hear God. I did not want to accept my marriage was failing, but God kept literally dropping receipts out of the sky, warning me our time was ending.

He made my comfort place so uncomfortable that I had to thirst for Him like never before. And so, in every uncomfortable situation God has placed me *in*, I began to trust that He would bring me *out*.

I trusted He knew all of the troubles I would face, but He also knew my unwavering faith in Him would unlock the next levels of blessings in my life. Each level was a training ground for the next.

I had to understand God always desired that I would have more, and, not only an abundance, but the best abundance He could provide. However, in order to receive God's best, I had to learn to move when told, listen attentively, and believe with everything in me that my best was yet to come. I became confident that whatever His will for my life was, that He was going to manifest it because my heart was now pure and open to Him.

Giving God my Isaac was not about giving Him my ex-husband, but giving Him *me*.

I learned how to walk in peace. Yes, I had days I wrestled with the 3-As: anxiety, anger, and acceptance, but I never lost sight of God.

My divorce was very public in the community in which we live, and, at first, it truly affected me. It affected my confidence, pride, and my heart, but I remember one day crying out to God asking, "Why did it have to be this way?" and, "Why couldn't I suffer in silence and seclusion?"

He replied: "I crucified you publicly so that the world would know your pain was real; you were left for dead, but I raised you on *purpose*."

Needless to say, I still do not know all my future holds, but I'm excited to see how all of this plays out! I'm excited about the new love that will come into my life, coupled with learning how to really walk in vulnerability and knowing my true worth and value.

Lastly, this book is not gender specific, but it's for people who are facing or who have faced pain and need direction on where to channel it. Healing and documenting it was my purpose, but feel free to insert your own experiences in your *Purposeful Pain* journal and watch God transform your entire being.

I thank you for being on this journey with me, and stay tuned because we've literally only just begun.

Love,
The Purposeful Woman

ABOUT THE AUTHOR...

L
AUREN GRIMES-JACKSON, author of Purposeful Pain *is first and foremost a Christian woman whose life is dedicated to helping broken women and men, through her own life experiences, journey toward wholeness. She is a successful entrepreneur in the arena of Mortgage Banking, having obtained a Master's Degree in Banking and Finance & an MBA, both from New England College, Henniker, New Hampshire. Lauren was born and reared in Opelousas, Louisiana, matriculated through Northwestern State University, Natchitoches, Louisiana, where she earned her Bachelor's degree; thereafter, she married and made her home in Shreveport, Louisiana. After eleven years of marriage, she divorced in 2019, and it was then that her Purpose was released.*

Lauren's aspiration is to promote healing and liberation from the perpetual cycle of brokenness often associated with the vagaries of life. She depicts stages of healing on Purpose in her book Purposeful Pain.

Dearest to her heart are her two young sons, Alan Duval Jackson III and Alex Lawrence Jackson, along with a host of family and friends.

Made in the USA
Lexington, KY
28 October 2019